MASTER BUILDER

FORTNITE
CREATIVE MODE

P9-CEH-083

Fly (Double-Tap)

MEMORY USED

0 100
100 100
18,675 100,000

The Essential Unofficial Guide

Screenshot © 2019, Epic Games, Inc.

This book is book is available in quantity at special discounts for your group or organization.
For further information, contact:

Triumph Books LLC
814 North Franklin Street
Chicago, Illinois 60610
Phone: (312) 337-0747
www.triumphbooks.com

Printed in U.S.A.
ISBN: 978-1-62937-755-1

Content packaged by Mojo Media, Inc.
Joe Funk: Editor
Samantha M Skinner: Writer
Jason Hinman: Creative Director
Jack Hinman, David Woodburn, Anderson Schlyer: Gaming Consultants

CONTENTS

OVERVIEW OF CREATIVE MODE

Creative Mode is the latest (and greatest) craze on the market currently. With many following Fortnite and all that comes with it, the ability to build and create something new is promising to many players. Others just want to be able to build without worrying about battle, since this can be frustrating during gameplay. By using Creative Mode, many players are able to practice their building without having to worry about being killed in the process. They can actually learn how to do so quickly and more efficiently, so perhaps they won't get killed the next time they head into battle. Others just use it to explore their creativity and test out new ideas.

Creative Mode has launched, and it has brought much more to the audience than the makers of Fortnite ever thought it would. It has a million different uses already and it has allowed the players to do something new with Fortnite and all the items that come in the game.

Many wonder what exactly this mode is and why does it matter for those of you that play Fortnite?

SEASON 7 BATTLE PASS

CREATIVE

Buy the Battle Pass and get early access to your island in Creative! You'll instantly unlock your own personal island, allowing you to save your creations. Don't just build, build your Fortnite with friends.

Creative will be free for all players on December 13.

• • • •

H Help   ESC Back

WHAT IS CREATIVE MODE ON FORTNITE?

Creative Mode is much like Roblox or Minecraft in the way that it works. It allows you to create and build anything you can think of. With an endless variety of materials and tools, you can build something that appeals to your own likes and wants. Not only that, but those that want to learn how to build faster and more efficiently are able to do so with the use of this mode as well. Everyone can benefit from this powerful new tool.

This part of the game was once only open and available to Battle Pass owners that wanted to expand their creativity or learn how to be better at playing the game. Now, it has opened up to everyone that plays the game,

regardless if they are a Battle Pass owner or not. This provides everyone with a chance to check it out and see what Creative Mode has to offer them.

Many players are already finding out that this is one of the easiest ways to build and you can create just about anything using the materials provided.

This mode allows players to create and forge their own island. Not only do you get a large space to work with, but you don't have to go around looking for supplies, they're provided for you, so you can be as creative as you would like without interruption or having to look around for materials to use. Set your mind free, test out your most creative ideas and marvel at what you're able to make. Before you know it you'll have a rich island designed exactly the way you want.

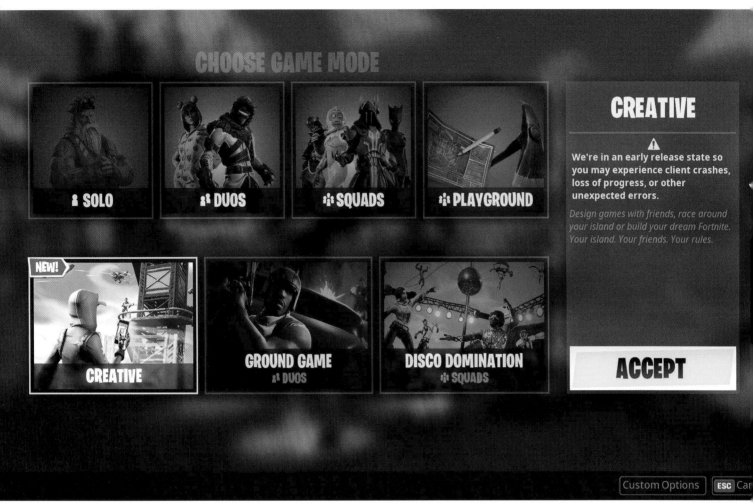

The island provides the user with a blank canvas to do all of the building that they want to do and to create something cool in the process. It's also a tool letting them learn how to build quickly and efficiently so they can go back and conquer Battle Royale.

Learning to build right away has been tough on a lot of the players. Many of them might be able to build something small and not so intricate, but others long to build something more. They want complete buildings that provide a place to hide and they're easy to make using Creative Mode. You can build faster, quicker and more efficiently in the game once you have paid a visit to your very own island.

Fortnite took their Creative Mode an extra step and provided the users with much more than just unlimited supplies. You can actually fly around the map wherever you want to go. They gave everyone even more tools to use that you cannot find in the game. You'll have all new ways to construct something new, and before you know it you can make something so original that you'll be amazed it's even made with Fortnite building blocks. This has opened a whole new world for players of the game and trust us, the world that you will fly around in on Creative Mode is quite massive in size.

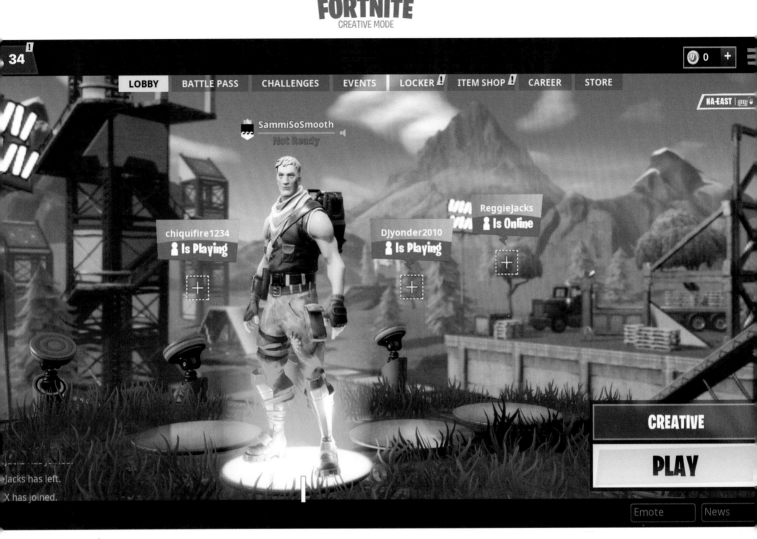

THE CREATIVE HUB

This is the first place that you'll see when you open up Creative Mode in the game. It is where you can get your creative juices flowing and make sure to prepare yourself for some pretty epic builds.

The moment you enter the hub you start off on a stone slab. This slab is surrounded by rocks that let you choose exactly where you want to go. The gold colored rock is the option to choose to go to the personal creation area, while the other stones let you visit friends or the coolest creations by other players that Epic wants to highlight and show off.

The Hub is not a very exciting or colorful area for you to visit, but it is one that provides you with an interactive menu, so you can choose where to go from here. The most important feature that you should know about the hub is that you can visit other people's creations through this area. This is where you will want to go when a friend says come check out my stuff or if you want to see which creation is on display through the company.

QUICK GUIDE

★ Gold stone lets you create your own world

★ Fortnite Island Codes are needed to share games between friends and other players

★ Fortnite community is found on one of the stones

★ Mini games can be accessed here

★ Previous builds and creations are shown in the rocks

Screenshot © 2019, Epic Games, Inc.

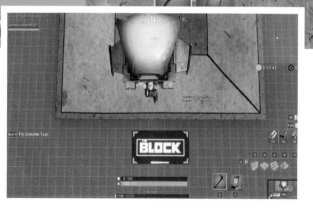

THE ISLANDS

Each player gets access to four different creative spaces that they can use. Each one of these spaces is called an island and they are quite literally, an island. It is a big open area that is surrounded by pretty mountains and that gives the player enough free space to build whatever they want to build on it. You can also name the islands whatever you want to name them, which is something that you can do just to tell the difference between the four when you're building something different on each of them.

You can build as much or as large as you like, but each island has its own memory limit attached to it and it will stop you once you hit or reach this limit. Once you hit your island's limit, you will get a prompt and it will save the island and your progress, so you can exit and come back later if you want.

Everything that is placed in your island can be manipulated and changed to your liking. If you want something specific, then you can use the prefabs that were made specific for this island and Creative Mode itself.

PREFABS

Prefabs are a powerful tool that lets you lay down whole buildings, monuments and towers with the click of a button. Imagine the Port-a-Fort but on a bigger scale and you'll start to understand this powerful feature. Whether you want to transform your island with entire buildings from Fortnite's Battle Royale, or you just want to speed up the building process prefabs will allow you to do just that. Grab parts of the game world you know such as Tilted Towers or those buildings that are found in Lucky Landing and get your ideal world up and running sooner.

You can grab furniture too! Just check out the fridge or the couch, a bed or a dresser, a bookshelf or anything else. Everything you can think of can be put into the game. You can spawn these things right into the game and then alter or copy them however you need them to be. This makes

adding things to the game, without having to make them from scratch, much simpler and easier for everyone involved.

You might be good at building, but with prefabs you won't have to build everything from scratch. Have fun making custom creations but speed up areas of your build using this cool feature and save your creativity for other areas of your island.

You don't have to just choose from objects and items either. You can go with walls or other parts of building that need to be used when you're constructing something that is going to be built up tall. You can choose the right building that keeps everyone safe inside. Just copy what you need and put it all together when the time comes to create a world that everyone loves.

TYPES OF GAME MODES

There are also different types of game modes that you can think about adding to the island that you are creating. Of course, this is not a must. You can choose to do whatever you would like with the island that they give you to create on. However, some like to create games of their own and Fortnite has created prefab games that players can choose from when they are creating their islands to add to the islands. This gives those going through the island with something to do and enjoy.

You can create an entire game that is custom-made around your custom-made map. This makes Creative Mode even more exciting.

You can choose from free-for-all deathmatches that you customize to your liking and bend the rules or give no rules at all, after all, it is your game board that you're messing with. You can also build a race course that you go through as fast as possible. It's your world, do whatever it is that will get your heart pumping and help you have fun with your friends.

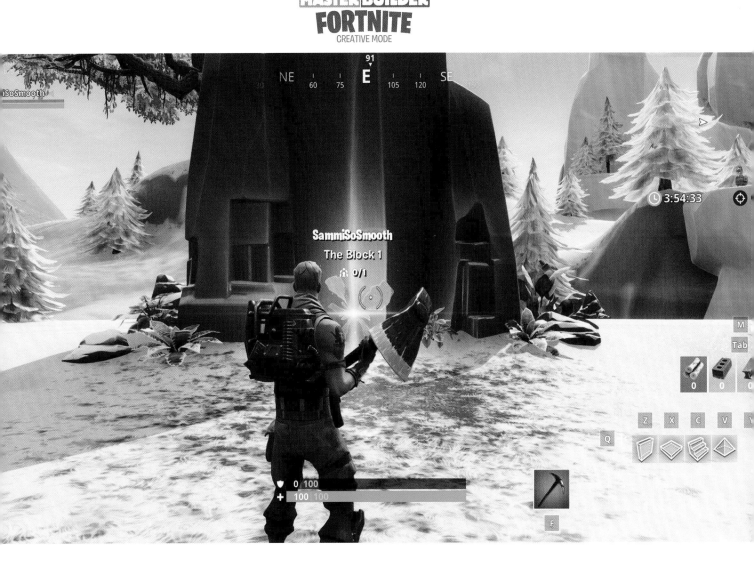

There are many types of games that you can use to your advantage when you're shuffling through everything in Creative Mode's prefabs and being able to choose what game you want to offer your players helps you create your ideal island. When they come into the island, they'll instantly see what you've put together, and if it's cool enough it might just become the destination they want to come back to again and again.

Speak with the players, learn what you can change and what they think about the map and the world you put together. You want them to love it, but you also want to make sure that you're not overdoing it. They can be the judges when they come in once you've developed a game system. Just make sure to play the game yourself to see how you feel about it, as well.

BRINGING PLAYERS TO YOUR ISLAND

Once you have created and crafted the island how you would like it to be, then you can actually invite up to 16 players to come out and visit. You can have them play Fortnite from a variety of match types, which allows them to have fun in your world but also play a game within it. This is offering much more than just building and enjoying a map of your own, it's experiencing it with others, which is the best way to play Creative Mode.

You don't have to invite just your friends from your friend's list to the island. You can open the world up to anyone that would like to come in and take a look. One of the other things about sharing the island is that if you think it is pretty awesome and you want to try to get it featured, then submit the island to the game makers to have them add it to Fortnite's main Battle Royale map. If you do end up making the cut and getting your creation in, it will show up with some of the others that also made it in a spot known as "The Block."

Be sure to only invite people that you trust because these players can walk around your island to wherever they would like to go and tweak and move designs to how they want them. Just keep this in mind when you invite others to your creative space and use permissions carefully to avoid serious problems with other players.

FLYING AROUND CREATIVE MODE

Many people do not realize that they can actually fly around in Fortnite's Creative Mode. You're easily able to get anywhere you want on the map with a simple click of the button. Just double tap the space bar and you're able to fly to wherever you want to fly.

This comes in handy when you're building something, and you want to look at it from afar. You can fly above it and then zoom out to see if everything is in place where it needs to be. It changes the perspective that you have while building and it can also come in handy when you're creating a game and you need to know what to do or where to go. You can see it all when you have eyes on top of the world to look down.

CREATIVE   PLAY

re | Consumable

ASTLE

ce a building in an instant

Prefabs   Devices   Weapons   Consumables   Chest

Equip

Add to Chest

ESC Back

CREATING OBSTACLES

This is Creative Mode and many think that they just come here to build. You don't just have to create pretty worlds though. You can create unique obstacle courses that will challenge other players. Put obstacles in place that others have to go over, under and around. There are plenty of actions that you can make people do or put in your world. This is ultimately like Roblox, where you can make just about anything happen.

This means that the island you're putting together is actually your island and you can make sure that you are getting all of the benefits that come from owning one of your own. It's exciting being able to develop it any way that you would like, so make the most of the experience.

Many have found that if they wanted to create a game of sorts through Creative Mode, they can actually create things that other players have to do. Once this is put into the system, they can test it before opening up their island to other players that like to visit many of the ones open. It is not only a great way to make friends and meet new people, but to really develop those gaming skills that might be useful later on if you want to create actual video games.

Creative Mode is offering a lot but being able to create obstacles and a game of your own is one of the biggest perks of using this mode over the others. Of course, you're going to want to go out and do some battle royales every now and again, but when you're ready to relax and work on your building Creative Mode will be there waiting for you!

IT LOOKS A LOT LIKE MINECRAFT

For all those Minecraft lovers out there that have ventured on to bigger and better things, you might just find a new love within the Fortnite walls with this new Creative Mode that everyone is now able to access.

When Fortnite gets regular updates, with a new season every 10 weeks, there is always bound to be something new and exciting to look at. This is what is making many of the players from other games, like Minecraft, turn their attention to Fortnite, even if they are not into the Survival Mode, or following a Story Mode.

Creative play is offering a brand-new experience and gameplay that is unlike any other. Fortnite's become the game to beat, and it continues to evolve into a more and more unique game with each passing month. What started off as what seemed like a PUBG clone with building, is now one of the most interesting gaming experiences that you'll witness today.

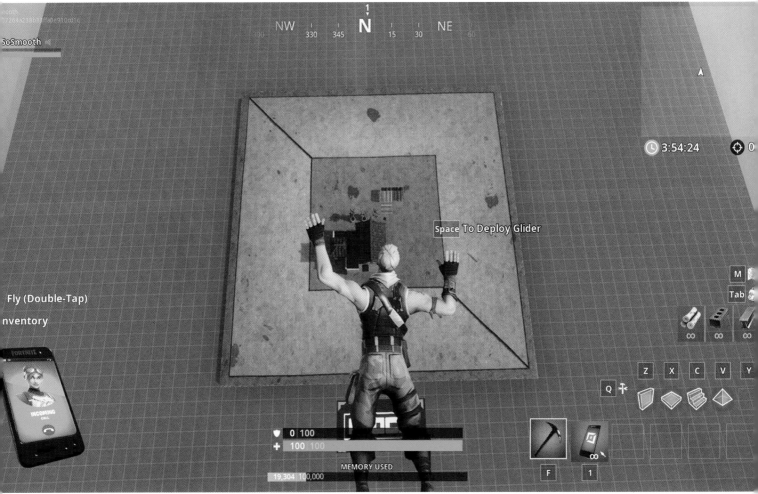

USE THE ADVANCED MENU AND CREATIVE BAR TO GET STARTED

While we'll dive deeper into all the features offered by the Creative Bar and the Advanced Menu, we'll start off by saying that you can create a variety of exciting features using the Creative Bar in this game mode. There are many buttons that you can push that give you different actions to make use of. Use the tools on this bar to manipulate the world and carefully place every object exactly where you want them.

Once you're more comfortable with all the basic tools on the Creative Bar, you can move on to the Advanced Building Menu and all the more involved tools included

there. Start practicing with these more difficult tools and you can really start creating something unique that will impress your visitors and let you express your creativity in Fortnite.

If you have something in mind, know that there are advanced features and tools that can be used to help you achieve the look that you want. You don't have to stick completely to the basic tools that are given on the main menu in the Creative Mode. You have the ability to do just about anything when you're building on Creative Mode in Fortnite.

WHAT YOU CAN DO

Fortnite's new Creative Mode gives you more ways to have fun than ever before. You can create to your heart's content, and you can experience all the fun with three of your best friends too! The Creative Mode was only open to those that had the Battle Pass, but now it has opened for everyone to use. If you love creating things, then this is the place for you to spread your creative wings and to begin forming your own world.

Creative Mode is a rich and engaging experience that's a lot of fun to play with. Each time you get onto your world you can expect to find plenty of things to keep you going, regardless of what you want to create and how you want to create it. Take a look at our quick-start guide to figure out how to make the most of Creative Mode. Skim through the guide for tips or read through each section and take your creative abilities to the next level.

Most new players start off wondering what's possible in Creative Mode, but they quickly go from wondering about the possibilities, to wondering how to do everything they want. There are simple commands giving you access to most of the game's items, as well as pre-built structures, boxes and powerups that you can use to create an exciting world that others want to experience.

Sound interesting? If you're ready to learn more, we're excited to teach you. Work with us to learn how to get the most out of Creative Mode, and quickly get up to speed in all the standard commands so you can maximize your fun with the game mode the next time you log on. Find out how to build something worth building.

THE NEW GAME MODE AND WHAT YOU WILL FIND INSIDE

This new game mode transforms Fortnite into something more similar to Minecraft or Roblox. So many have explored the depths of the rich Story Mode, and players are all familiar with the intensity of the Battle Royale mode, but Creative Mode is something different entirely. It gives you the freedom to think, to invent and to build your own new exciting world. Make your own games, make your own islands and show them off to everyone that you know.

Creative Mode is arguably one of the biggest and most exciting additions made to Fortnite. The creators of the hit game are constantly making new enhancements, but few will transform the way you play like Creative Mode does.

That's why Creative Mode has received all the attention that it has. Players are responding in a big way, and that's no surprise to us.

This new game mode is sure to take the world by storm. Many players that didn't like the other aspects of the game will find themselves being drawn in by Creative Mode. It's a much different experience that Battle Royale or even Save the World. It's more open, creative and inventive.

Creative Mode is off to a big start and everyone is invited to come inside and check out all that comes with this new game mode and what you can get from it.

Build your own Fortnite! Everything you do here is saved.

GETTING CREATIVE MODE FOR YOURSELF

Once only available to those that held the Battle Pass, Creative Mode has recently been opened to every player around the world. It is available as one of the free game options and it is better than many players could have ever expected.

You're able to race, to beat obstacles, to have battles and even fly with planes. The choice is yours on what you decide to make and how the entire game looks. You can unleash your creativity any way you like. If you've ever thought about a way to improve upon Fortnite, now's your chance. Take those hidden ideas and bring them to life in your very own world!

When you go to the **Main Menu** of the game under Battle Royale where you can choose what type of game you want to play, you just have to select **Creative Mode out of the available game types.** This is where you can choose to open up one of your saved islands, a new island, visit a friend's island with a code, or you can visit the community where people have their islands open for everyone to come in and check them out. Your current selection is displayed by the stones around the pad that you stand on.

Once in the creative area, you're on your own island. You can name it whatever you want and make it look however you like. Create a world of your own and the rules can also be anything you want them to be. It is your world entirely, from how you play the game to how it looks.

Remember, you don't get an unlimited number of islands or space, so think about what you want to build. Of course you're free to delete an island and start over again, but be aware that you'll wipe out all your progress if you do. Everyone gets 100,000 points of memory space and four different islands that they can develop and make into anything that they want. However, when these are filled up, they are gone. You either have to stop playing in Creative Mode or you have to delete the stuff off of one of your existing islands to create something new in the same area.

WHAT CREATIVE MODE ISN'T GOING TO TELL YOU

Creative Mode is a mode that you jump into and have to figure out for yourself. There are no guides or tutorials that give you information on what you should be doing or how to do it. That's why it's so helpful to have a guide like ours to help you get started and to give you some ideas to get you going.

While Fortnite doesn't hide things from you, they certainly do not come out and show you what you should be doing. That's why it's important to think creatively, to look at what others have done with Creative Mode and to decide what you want to do on your own islands.

The first thing you should know about Creative Mode is that you can change permissions for each of the guests that come and visit your islands. These permissions give you control over who does and does not change, move, remove, and add to the world around you. You can make changes through the menu, which we will explain below.

The next most important thing you should know about is how to access your inventory out in the world. You do so through the phone that is provided on the menu bar. This doesn't allow you to put new items in the world, but it can help you place, move, remove, turn and perform other functions with the current items that you have and those in the world. For example, if a tree is in your way, you can use the phone to move it for you.

If you're looking for a way to put new things into your island, then make sure to take a look at the prefabs, because this is where you will find the buildings, weapons, items and more.

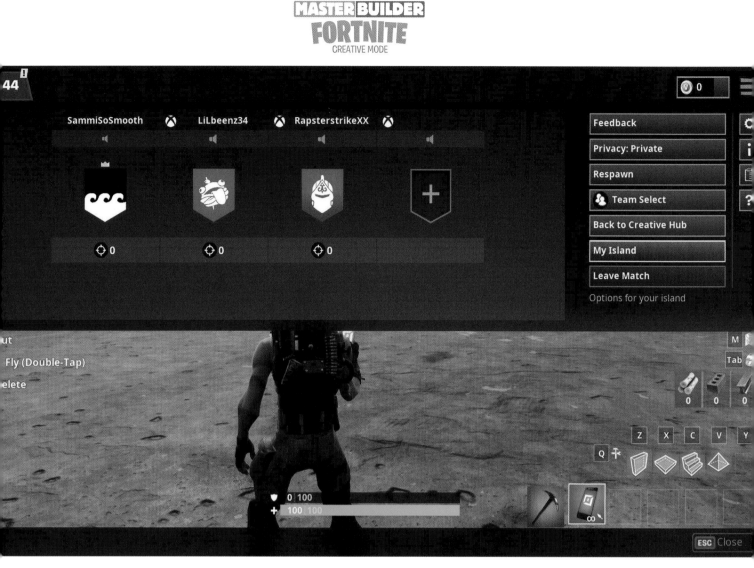

MORE DETAILS ON GIVING PERMISSIONS

If you invite friends to your island, you may want them to build alongside you. This is okay, and it is something that can be done, but you have to change the permissions to allow them to do so. The same goes for players looking to protect their creations from random players that enter their islands.

These permissions can all be adjusted to meet your needs through the menu.

> Open up the **Main Menu** — this menu is where you can also exit the game, change your video settings and see player stats

> Go to the **My Island** option shown towards the bottom of the screen

> Click on **Island Tools** to be brought to the options you need

> There will be two options, you want to choose the **Island Edit Permission.** Then you can change the options from **Only Me** to **Everyone** or the other way around depending on which you want

Uncommon | Trap x5
DAMAGE TRAP
Trap | Floor
★★

| Arming Delay | 1.0 seconds |
| Reload Time | 5.0 seconds |

Creative Play

Prefabs **Devices** Weapons Consumables Chest

Equip   **Add to Chest**

ESC B

Once you give them permissions, they can start building right alongside you and help bring your ideas to life while adding some of their own. Remember how permissions work and how to use them and you'll never have to suffer with players editing parts of your world you don't want edited.

LEARNING HOW TO BUILD

One of the most important aspects of Creative Mode is building. That is the whole point of this new game mode. There aren't many limits to what you can do creatively. You can create your own games, your own area, mimic actual places and more. Take the time to get to know how each of the tools works and what you can do with them, then build to your heart's content and bring your ideas to life.

The **phone** tool in the **Main Menu,** as mentioned above, is not used to place new items inside the world, but is quite useful when you want to move, remove, change, duplicate or rotate anything that is already in the world. The phone tool is especially handy when trying to move something out of the way when you want to place a prefab down.

To get new items for your island, you have to go to the **inventory** that is provided in the main menu. The menu looks the same as the one that you have in Battle Royale. There are tabs at the top that you can look through based on what you need. It offers weapons, devices, prefabs, consumables, and chests to choose from.

Prefabs are something you will likely make use of a lot. Instead of having to create things from scratch, these provide you with a way to look through the options, click on what you want and then place it into the island easily and efficiently.

The inventory is where you'll find all the different items and structures offered throughout Fortnite's Battle Royale mode. This is where you can search for traps and everything else you're interested in. The in-depth menu provides those that want to build with plenty of options to keep them building for hours. Just remember that the structures work the same way that they do inside the game. If you build a tall wall and then remove the supports from the bottom, the entire wall is going to fall down around you.

To use prefabs and other items, just place them down on the floor like you are setting up a Port-a-Fort and you're set to go! Use the **phone** to move the object once it has been set on the island or to rotate, duplicate or change it in other ways.

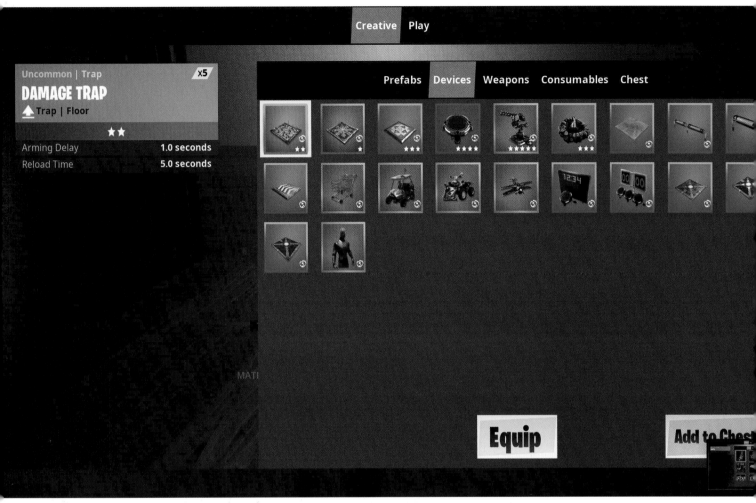

CHOOSING THE WEAPONS AND BUILDINGS YOU WANT ON YOUR ISLAND

Creative Mode in Fortnite comes with so many options that you might find yourself overwhelmed trying to figure out which you want to put on your island. Rest assured, we're here to help!

Look through the different buildings offered for that perfect structure. Do you have a favorite from Battle Royale? Do you want one that is a specific size or type? Look through the long list of options and you're bound to find one that will work perfectly for your needs.

The prefabs tab provides endless building options and you just have to scroll through them to find the right one for your needs.

The weapons tab provides the builder with every single weapon that you can find in Battle Royale, except for the Infinity Blade because it is so new that they didn't want to give that one away just yet. You can have any of the others spawn where you need them to, though.

You can set up spawns across your map, and even build specialized crates that show up around your map to give players what they need and to make interesting game modes of your own design. You just have to go through a couple of steps and you're set to rock and roll.

> Pull up the **inventory** where you have access to everything you need to build on your island

> **Scroll** to the right until you've reached the weapons page, this is where you can take weapons to add to your arsenal or to a chest or llama, depending on your needs

You can also use this function to put different items in your game, like chests, consumables or other items. The chests and llamas that you put into the game can hold up to 50 items each, but you don't have to choose that many if you don't want.

The tools and inventory provide the user with eight different obstacle courses they can choose from, 25 different buildings that were chosen and placed in the inventory from Battle Royale and 34 galleries of building tiles and props to select from. The makers of Creative

Mode wanted to make sure that whatever the players wanted to make, they were able to. They added in the ability to create freely and give all the options you might want in terms of weapons and consumables.

Use all of the options provided to maximize your game's potential. Epic has really thought of everything to grab your interest and bring out the creativity that you have hiding within.

25

THE MEMORY THAT YOU GET WITH YOUR ISLAND

Everyone starts off with a specific amount of memory that they can use to build on their island with. You're given 100,000 memory points to do with what you please. There is a bar at the bottom of the screen that provides you with a way to keep track of how much memory you have already used and how much you have left.

When you start a new island, you will notice that it uses about 9,200 memory. This is because of the trees, rocks, grass and other features that are located around the island. If you want to get more memory to use on other things, just go around the island removing these items. It can give you almost 10,000 more memory to use on other things.

You might want to keep some of them and that is fine, but the more stuff left on the island, the more memory these items are going to take away from the build and the other items you can add to use to your advantage.

Here is an example of what you can expect when adding items to your island and how those items affect your total memory count. This quick guide will help explain what items use up the most memory and which ones are cheap to add to your world.

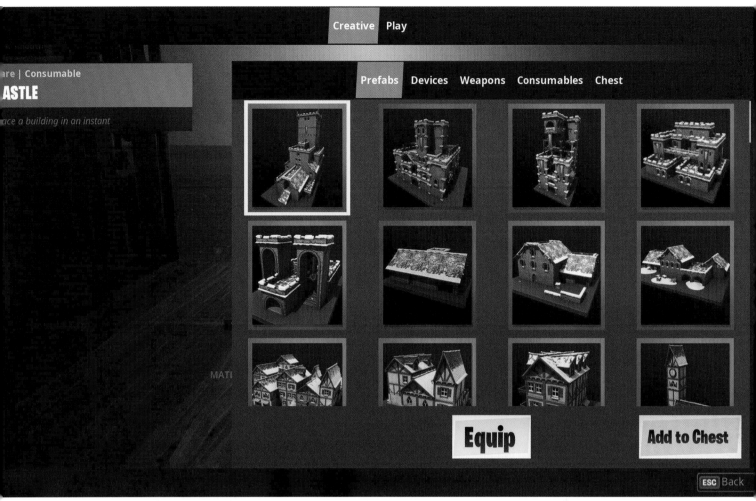

Creative   Play

are | Consumable

ASTLE

ace a building in an instant

Prefabs   Devices   Weapons   Consumables   Chest

Equip   **Add to Chest**

ESC Back

MATI

Prefab	Memory Used for the 1st Time	Memory Used for the 2nd Time
Gas Station	4,871	254
Cars	20	
Temple from Lucky Landing	17,500	830
Jump Pad	20	
Trees	4	

The cool thing about these prefabs is that they do not take up as much space the second time or third time that you use them. The most is used when you put it down for the first time.

EDITING ISLAND CODES FOR YOUR BENEFIT

Creative Mode allows players to create their own scenes. This means being able to edit and change many different parts of the world other than just weapons and standard building. By making a game that others can play, you might want the island to be able to do specific things, but to do this you'll need to understand how to edit island codes effectively.

Begin by going to the **Creative Hub** where you can **Start a Server** with a party or by yourself. This is where you can access your own private island.

In order to enter into one of the custom worlds provided, you have to walk over to the rifts, but don't walk through them. When you go up to them, an option window should pop up which wants you to enter an Island Code into the box. You can use your editor to input the code.

A new window is then going to open up and ask you to enter a new 12-digit code. This is a code that is given to the publisher of an island that they can share with others that they want to come in and show their island to. Any island that you are trying to reach should have a code that comes with it. Enter a friend's code in and you'll be taken straight to their island.

Once you enter the code into the box, they will give you a clip of how the island looks, the specs on it, the title and description. Click on the island to go to it. From there, you are sent to the island. Keep in mind that if the creator used a lot of the memory that the island comes with then it might take some time to fully load.

Run through the rift and you're set to go! Check out any and all of the islands that you have codes to with this awesome feature!

HOW TO TURN REPLAY ON AND OFF

Replay is a great feature for those that want to record everything that happens in their island. You already know that this feature is pretty cool when you are trying to re-watch some of your favorite kills or moves you made in the game, but it's something you can use in Creative Mode as well, so when people come and do something awesome during the game, you can catch it on camera. Learn to use the tool and you'll have plenty of footage to watch later!

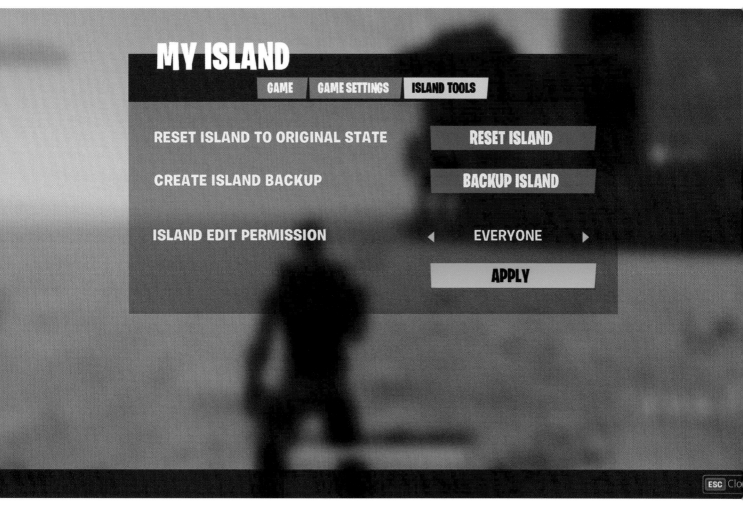

Just a few steps can help you turn the Replay feature on or off.

> Go to the **home** screen and open the **settings** option

> Scroll to the bottom of the settings

> This is where you will find the option to turn Replay **on** or **off**

It is not automatically turned on, so if you want to use it, then you will have to go through these steps to try and turn it on. Once it's on you'll have the ability to record important moments whenever you like.

DELETING YOUR ENTIRE ISLAND

If you're tired of a new island, or you were just using it as a testing ground and you're ready to move on, instead of trying to clean out an entire island, you can go ahead and delete the whole thing. Deleting a full island is the fastest way to clear up space and to give yourself a fresh start to play around with once again. Once you understand how, you can delete an island in mere minutes.

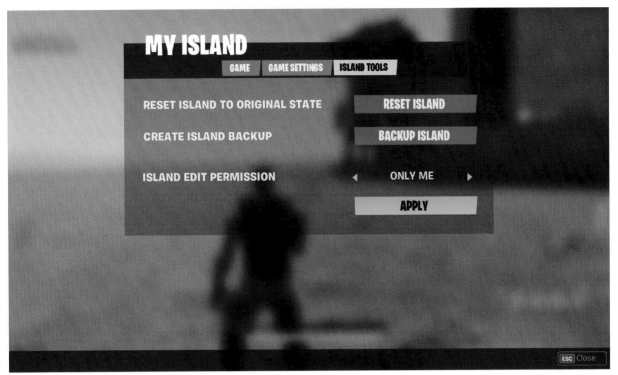

Start over fresh using these deets:

> Go to the **Main Menu** where the player stats and exit is located, and choose **My Island,** located at the bottom of the menu

> Click on the option tab named **Island Tools**

> Then you can click on the option that says **Reset Island to Original State,** click on the **Reset Island** option and you're set to go!

Everything will then be swept away just like that. Don't worry though, you will be moved too but will respawn near the exit rift on the screen. We're sure your mom probably wishes your room got clean just as fast!

If you're ready to build, then so are we. Make sure to consider the things you want to build on your island and that you have an idea of how it should look. From there you shouldn't have a problem piecing the map together.

Creative Mode seemingly showed up out of thin air. Its sudden arrival isn't holding people back though. As soon as it was up and ready to go, many people put their creative hats on and started building their own epic worlds, even though they didn't know what they were doing at first. They were ready to take on anything. If you are ready to start building and making your own game, then we are going to go over some specifics to help you create a game that will impress your friends and make them want to come back to your island again and again. If you want to make something up, be creative, add a new prefab with a specific game and more, you can do all those things, just take a moment with us to learn what you're doing...

You have the ability to do just about anything you can think of with Fortnite's Creative Mode. Epic Games has even invited players to share their most impressive creations with the world! Submit yours if you think you have what it takes to stand out and really give a game and island that is just as awesome as it can be. When you're ready to take the next step, we'll be waiting to guide you on your journey. Enjoy playing with all the new features offered on your own custom island, and get creative with Fortnite!

EXPLORE YOUR CREATIVE OPTIONS!

SELECT A SERVER

FERBUCHON

4/16

START A SERVER

LAUNCH

CANCEL

With all that is offered inside Creative Mode – You're the Master Builder of the Island!

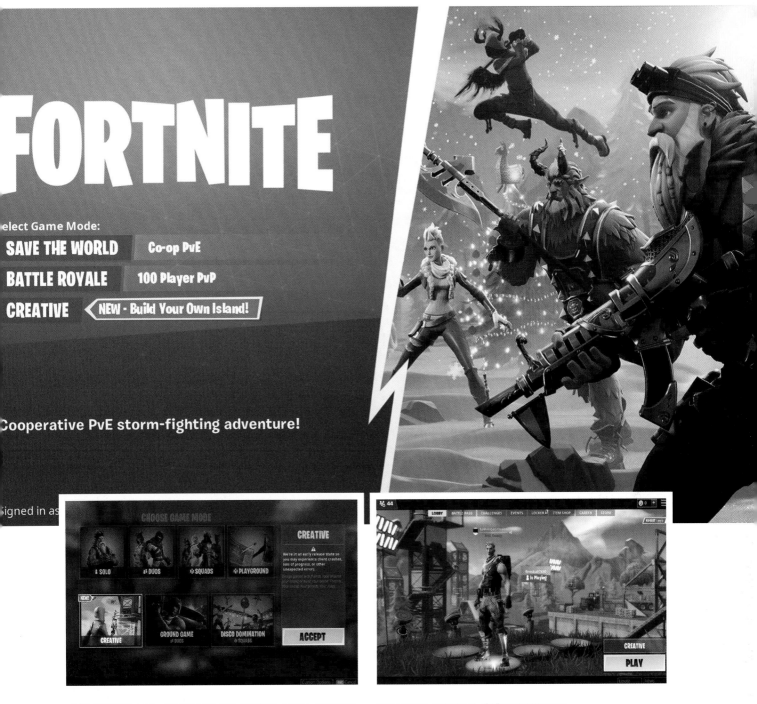

FORTNITE

elect Game Mode:

SAVE THE WORLD — Co-op PvE

BATTLE ROYALE — 100 Player PvP

CREATIVE — NEW - Build Your Own Island!

Cooperative PvE storm-fighting adventure!

igned in as

CREATIVE MODE IS THE NEWEST ADDITION TO FORTNITE

Everyone has access to the fun that awaits in Creative Mode, offering the ability to build a game of your own.

YOUR NEW CREATIVE ADVENTURE AWAITS

Enter into an island of your own and think about the many things that can be done to create a world all your own.

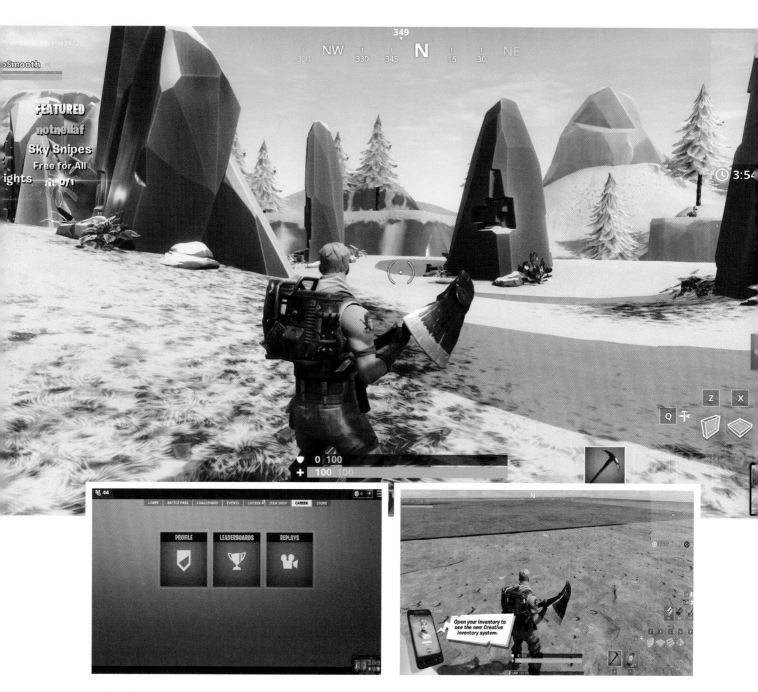

YOUR DESTINATION IS HIDDEN IN THE STONES

Choose where you'd like to go: to a friend's island, your own island or one of the featured islands offered by other players.

BUILDING A WORLD IS RIGHT AT YOUR FINGERTIPS

Use the phone to move, add, remove and change the many things that can be added to your island to create something unique.

THERE IS MORE THAN WHAT MEETS THE EYE

The middle of the island is a block, but there is so much more room for you to use when you explore a bit more.

THE GAME BEGINS WITH YOU

In Creative Mode, you are the master of the game because you are the only one creating it from how it looks to what you're supposed to do inside.

SELECT A SERVER

'GR	DIESELDO131	FATALKHAN561398	FLASHGORDONRO846	COOLESTDUDE53	JESUSTHEBIRD345	LZYDZYOOO
	0/16	3/16	6/16	3/16	2/16	1/16

LAUNCH

CANCE

CHOOSE YOUR OWN OR SOMEONE ELSE'S

You can go into someone else's world or game, or you can keep crafting your own.

CREATING YOUR OWN ISLAND

This is one of the best ways to get to expand your creative mind and really make something that people like.

CHOOSE YOUR OWN ROCK

If you are working on your own island, going to The Block is the option you should choose.

ENTERING YOUR ISLAND WITH A BURST

There's a burst of light once you choose your rock and go to your island, which is pretty cool.

MAKE AN ISLAND ALL YOUR OWN

Your island can look and work however you want, but you have to use some creative juices when considering how you want the game to be.

YOU ARE THE ONLY BOSS IN TOWN

When you enter the island, it is going to be a ghost town because you are the only one that is in the game at the moment.

YOU CAN ADD FRIENDS TO HELP

If you don't want to be the only one in town, just share your code with friends who can come help you build an island and a game.

MAKE THE ISLAND LOOK HOW YOU WANT

Of course, when you are in charge, you can build your own buildings or use the prefabs. Mix and match so it is set up however you want.

MASTER BUILDER
FORTNITE
CREATIVE MODE

THE PHONE IS FOR MORE THAN CALLS

The phone has a lot of useful tools that you can use to remove, edit, move, change and do anything you want to what is placed on the board, even prefabs.

READ THE TIPS THAT COME UP

The phone also comes with useful tips and tricks while you are putting your island together to make things easier.

Screenshots © 2019, Epic Games, Inc.

40

RIP APART PREFABS

The prefabs can have everything inside them stripped so you can have them bare from the inside out.

ALTER PREEXISTING BUILDINGS TO HOW YOU WANT

You can change the preexisting buildings however you want. You can even change the walls and duplicate them to give them a brand-new appearance.

MASTER BUILDER
FORTNITE
CREATIVE MODE

EVEN THE SMALLEST ITEMS ARE INSIDE

The items that you would notice in Battle Royale for the prefab buildings are also inside the buildings you put on your build.

TAKE A LOOK AROUND

Look around at everything on your island that you have put there and see what you need and what you don't need.

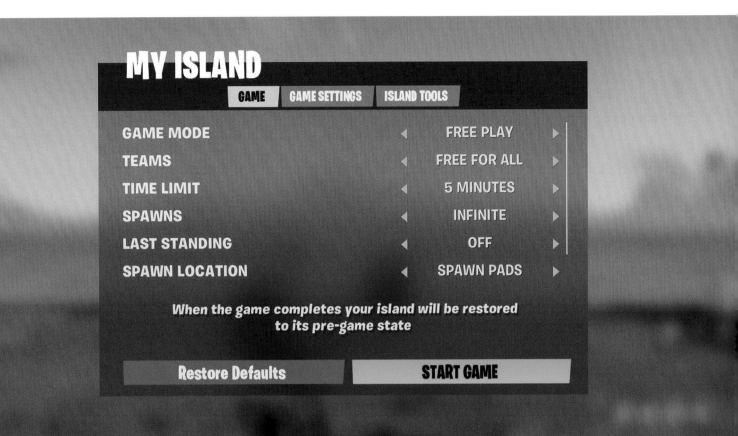

MY ISLAND

GAME   GAME SETTINGS   ISLAND TOOLS

GAME MODE	◄	FREE PLAY ►
TEAMS	◄	FREE FOR ALL ►
TIME LIMIT	◄	5 MINUTES ►
SPAWNS	◄	INFINITE ►
LAST STANDING	◄	OFF ►
SPAWN LOCATION	◄	SPAWN PADS ►

When the game completes your island will be restored to its pre-game state

Restore Defaults   **START GAME**

ESC Close

SET THE GAME HOWEVER YOU WANT

The game has many settings and controls that allow you to change out each of them however you'd like.

YOU CAN CONTROL HOW THE GAME IS PLAYED

These options don't seem like much but changing just a few of them can completely alter the game you put together.

THE GAME BEGINS WHEN YOU SAY

You can choose when to put the game together and then press start. Once in the game, you have to finish or log out of it.

SPAWN IN AN OUTSIDE LOCATION

The best part is that you can spawn randomly in the game, in the middle of the island or over on the spawn pad outside the island itself.

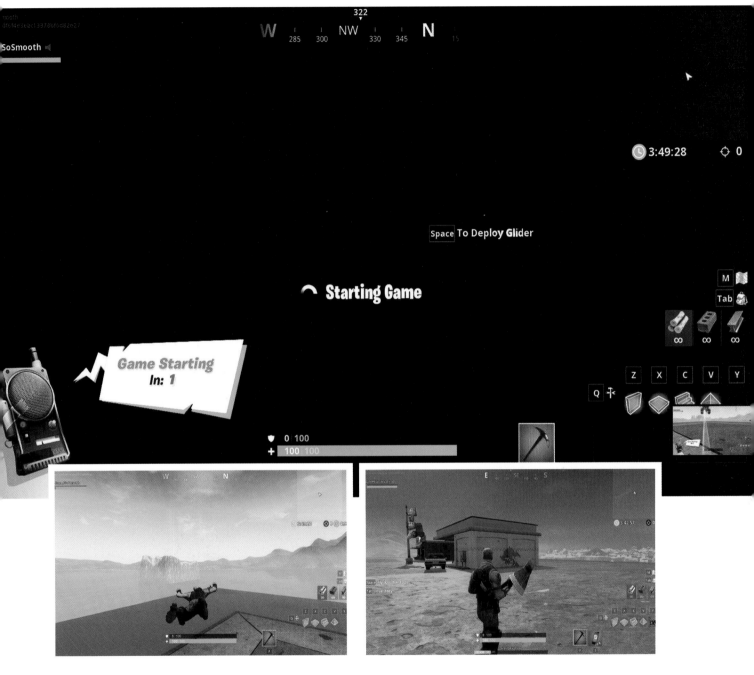

RESTART THE ISLAND

You can completely delete and restart the island build if you don't like what you made the first time around.

SIMPLY RESPAWN BACK

You can then just respawn back to The Block and on the spawn location.

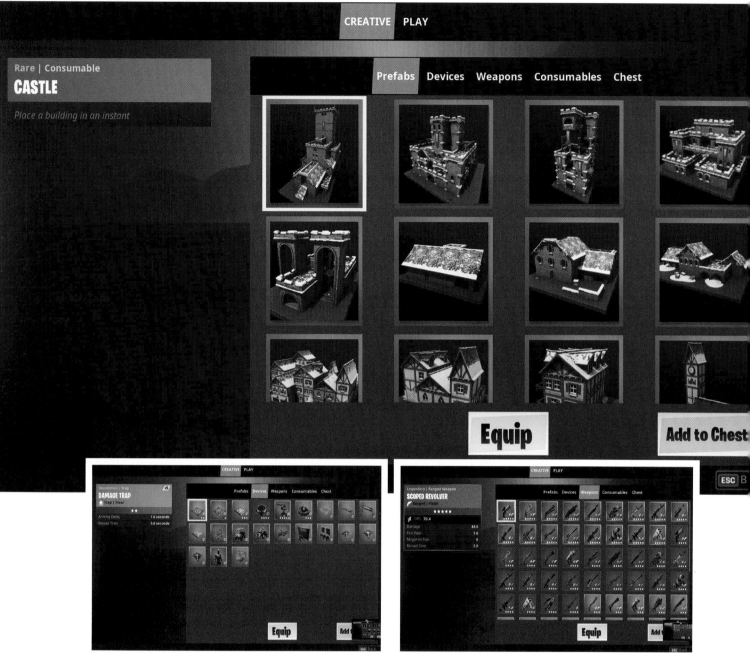

ADD ITEMS IN THE ISLAND

The inventory is full of so many things that you can add into your game to make it more enjoyable.

ADD PREFAB BUILDINGS, WEAPONS AND MORE

You can choose what to make and put in the island. Build obstacle courses or towns, create piñatas or chests, you have the ability to do it all.

MASTER BUILDER
FORTNITE
CREATIVE MODE

CREATIVE PLAY

mmon | Ranged Weapon   x5

RENADE

Ranged | Explosive Weapon

★

PS   100.0

mage   100.0

Prefabs   Devices   Weapons   **Consumables**   Chest

Equip

Add t

ESC Back

CREATIVE PLAY

Legendary | Trap

QUADCRASHER SPAWN
🔺 Trap | Floor

LV 1/10

Arming Delay   0.0 seconds
Reload Time   1.0 seconds
Start Time   0.0 seconds
Critical Hit Chance   0%
Durability   24

Prefabs   Devices   Weapons   Consumables   Chest

Equip   Add to Chest

ESC Back

FIND THE TRAPS AND MORE

The Cozy Campfire and Disco Ball traps can even be found and then strategically placed throughout the island for the players.

CREATE A LOOT CRATE ALL YOUR OWN

Hide one of the best loot crates anywhere on the island's map. Choose a crate and then fill it with everything imaginable.

PLACE BUILDINGS ANYWHERE

You can place buildings anywhere you want on your square.

WATCH FOR THE GREEN SQUARE

When the green square lights up, that is where the building is going. You throw it there and it builds.

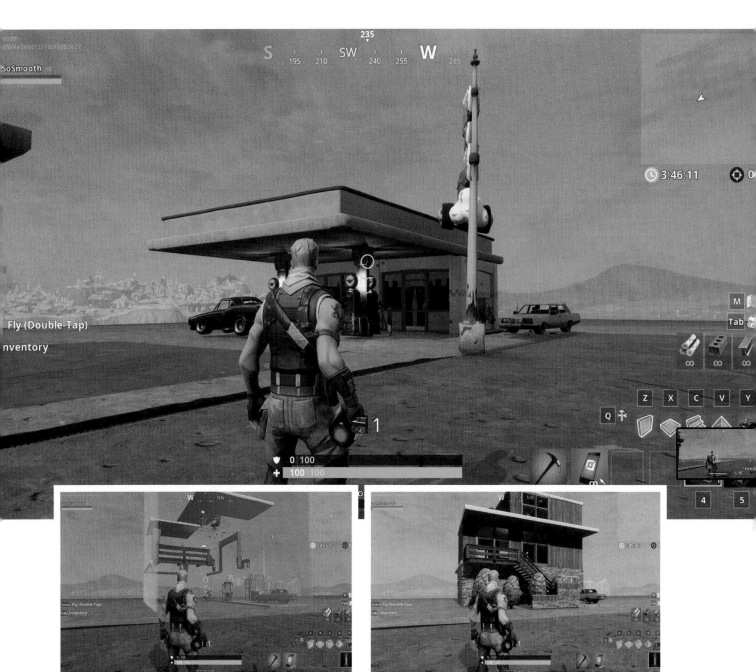

BUILDING IS EASY

You don't have to do anything fancy to build something on the island. You just throw the ball and it happens.

IT TAKES JUST SECONDS!

Once thrown onto the spot that you choose, the building is up within seconds, so there is no waiting long periods for a build to happen.

YOU CAN CREATE A WHOLE MAP

Create a map of your own. With buildings that work, weapons and more, you can create a Grand Theft type of game, a maze and more.

MAKE A TOWN

Minus the people, until you give out the code to your world. You just have to come up with an objective for them to play through.

PLAY HOUSE

Complete with weapons while you scope out the competition that is coming your way!

CREATE A GAME

The game is based on traps and resources being scarce and everyone not having enough of everything to make it through – this makes it more exciting!

★★★ THEMES

Everyone has a vision they want to bring to life, and with Fortnite Creative Mode you can flex your creative muscles and create your own world... With plenty of prefabs, weapons, tools and more, you can design unique mini games, or just build for fun. Fortnite provides you with everything you need to create - just make sure you don't outdo Fortnite's Battle Royale!

Building is something many players can really excel with. Whatever it is that you want to create, you can find all the tools you need in Creative Mode. You can easily transform that empty piece of island into whatever it is you want. Not only that, but if you design your island with a fun theme, everyone is going to want to show up at your island to check out the land and the game that awaits them.

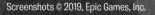

GAME THEMES TO CHOOSE FROM

Knowing what types of games you can make your map into is important. Having a clear vision allows you to build a theme around the type of game you wish to create.

When starting a new creation, you have a few pre-designed games to pick from, or you can create something entirely unique, the choice is yours! Have fun and get creative, you never know what you'll come up with if you make the most of your creative freedom.

Obstacle Course

An obstacle course is an entertaining game type many creators are designing their worlds around. Add in tough obstacles, intricate climbing platforms and hidden traps to keep things interesting. There are so many tools available that you really can create any obstacle configuration you like, so make it as challenging or as easy as you want.

In the Prefabs section, you will find numerous obstacle courses to choose from. Not only can you use the pre-build obstacles, but you can take out the AR phone and make custom modifications to the prefabs. So, get to ripping those things apart and making something new! With prefabs and unique building blocks you can create that perfect structure that fits your design idea.

Creative   Play

Rare | Ranged Weapon
PHONE
Ranged

★★★★   LV 1 / 1

DPS 0.0

Damage	0.0
Fire Rate	0.0
Magazine Size	1
Reload Time	0.0

Traps & Resources

Ammo

Equipment

Death Matches

Death matches are very much like what you would find on Battle Royale, except you call the shots and make the rules. You can have even teams, one against many, or any configuration that you like, you name it. It's you're world. Design the death match any way you like and head into battle with your friends, or complete strangers!

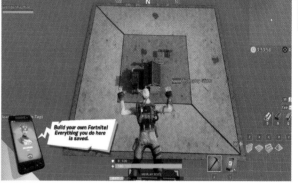

Of course, before you can do all those cool customizations, you need to understand the settings and the tools. We will explain exactly how to create the best match that you can, even if it ends up being something unique and not a death match at all. Keep reading and learn about match settings and how to make those important customizations.

Use "My Island" in the Main Menu to share and change settings.

CHANGE MATCH SETTINGS TO MAKE THE ULTIMATE MINI GAME

The match settings are important. When you want to have the ultimate mini game, you have to think of the features that will make it challenging. There are a variety of settings you can adjust to alter your game and the world itself. With different settings that you can adjust, you can choose the features that will make your game stand out. Of course, how you set it up and how it looks is also just as important, so you'll have to keep the appearance in mind as well whenever you change up the settings. Think about the map you've already created, and how any new changes will affect your creation.

When you hit the **ESC** button on your keypad, the **Main Menu** will pop up on the screen. Once there, choose the **yellow button** called **My Island.** You can use this to change the **team rules** and **match settings** for your island. When creating the ultimate in Fortnite mini games, the main menu will give you access to all the most important features to help you along.

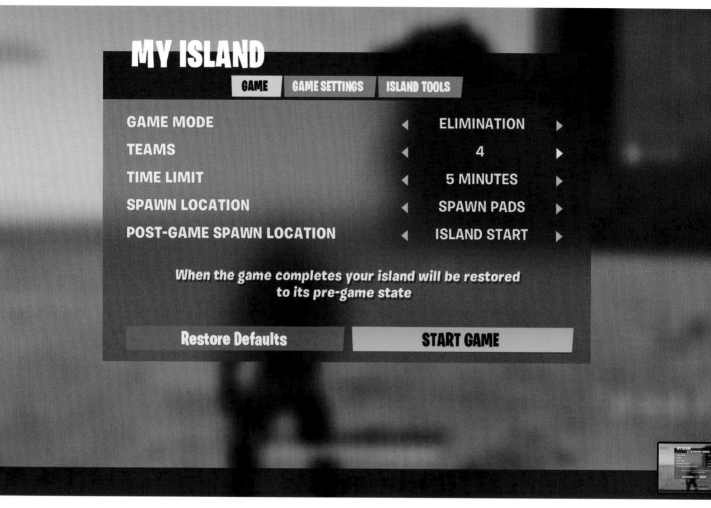

You can choose to tweak just about everything, except for how the game looks. Here are some of the things you can adjust to your liking using the built-in settings:

- Game Mode
- Teams
- Time Limit
- Spawn Location

You can customize just about every aspect of the game you want. From the life you want to give everyone to the shields they can use. You can let 2 teams play, PvP, 4 teams or a free for all. You have the ability to create the ultimate game.

What's more is that you get to choose what is in the game for players to use. If you want 6 players to come and play, but you only put 3 guns in the entire game, you'll have players scrambling for weapons and an interesting battle to the death that's more than a little one-sided!

Crafting your own mini games is the perfect way to get more familiar with Fortnite's Creative Mode, and even to improve some of your fighting skills along the way. Mini games are a perfect way to explore many of the options available in Fortnite's Creative Mode. These games are the perfect way to express yourself. If you're not big into coding and creating apps and games, you can enjoy creating without having to learn those new skills. It's easy to sign up and get going.

MY ISLAND

GAME | **GAME SETTINGS** | **ISLAND TOOLS**

GAME MODE	◄	ELIMINATION	►
TEAMS	◄	4	►
TIME LIMIT	◄	NONE	►
SPAWN LOCATION	◄	SPAWN PADS	►
POST-GAME SPAWN LOCATION	◄	ISLAND START	►

When the game completes your island will be restored to its pre-game state

Restore Defaults | **START GAME**

ESC | Close

Each island supports up to four squads of four. You can adjust these numbers too, but the pre-set lobby size is 16. Depending on your game type, you can reduce the number of players allowed on your island too, you have creative control!

There are so many different creative options available, but it's up to you to adjust them to your liking to get the best outcome. Some players even theme their games around other games, movies or situations that they have seen. You can do this, or you can come up with something new and entirely different.

Then, once you're done, showcase them online for one and all to look at. This makes searching for your own game, as well as any others you want to use as inspiration, easy to do. Just go to the website and search through the available games that are being offered.

Jot down their code and go to the crystals that are standing up by your crystal to get into your island. Once there, input the code for the island you want to visit. There is no limit in the number of places you can visit either. This means you can spend your entire day looking at the islands that others have put together and then made public for everyone to see (public and private options are both available in the game mode settings).

You're free to create your world any way you like, but it's a good idea to think about what others are playing to create a world that's going to appeal to a large group of players. Everyone is different and what one person likes might not be something that another person would like to play. If you're just making the island for fun and are not creating a game or are going to keep it private, then you don't have to worry about any of this. You can just build to your heart's content.

Once you've created something you love, you're free to share it with friends or the public, or you can keep it all to yourself. If you do decide to share it, do so by showing off your world's code. Once they have your code they can hop into your world and see what you've made. Who knows, you could build up a following all your own!

Have fun when creating and don't worry about making a game that's going to appeal to everyone. Create something that you love, enjoy the experience, and maybe others will love it just as much as you!

WHAT OTHER PLAYERS HAVE THOUGHT UP

There are already thousands of unique worlds that have shown up overnight since the Game Mode was launched. People are showcasing their creativity and frankly it's a lot of fun looking at all these unique worlds. Below are some cool examples we witnessed while looking through some new worlds. Use them for inspiration for what you can create yourself.

Of course, these are going to change from time to time because there are always new games coming up and when they reach a large number of viewers, they are then showcased on the website. Find out which ones make the cut and see how long you can get yours up there. This is the ultimate challenge, not having to stay alive before the storm or another player gets you but being able to have your island showcased on The Block.

Have you ever wanted to have a death match on a bounce pad? That's a cool idea that one player came up with. Now you and your friends can fight it out like you're battling on top of a giant trampoline.

How about battling inside a cube that doesn't have windows or doors for you to move in and out of? It's a unique concept that keeps fighting very close range, it's also a way to practice fighting right next to your enemy.

There's another game that focuses on the best snipes made, and one made just from toys.

You can go with a constant motion arena that always has you spinning and being on your toes or mirrors everywhere you turn. There is something for everyone and you can add to that fun with some of your own crazy ideas.

Not only are players creating their own unique places, but some are re-creating well-known areas from other games. There are maps that mirror maps from Halo for example. There are plenty of other cool examples straight from popular video games showing up on Fortnite islands. If there's something you believe is missing from Fortnite, now's your chance to bring it straight into the game.

No matter what you want to create, you can do just that on your island. It's an exciting time to be a Fortnite player, and you really can use any theme that you like. Use popular islands as your own personal source of inspiration, copy the aspects you like and make unique additions to make them even better. There's no reason you can't make a top island, you just have to take a good theme and make it your own. Get out there and get creating and you might be impressed with what you can create.

YOUR GAME CAN REALLY ROCK

The game that you choose to make is all your own but getting your island to The Block is difficult. Many players build just for the specific goal of getting their game on this piece of land on the map.

Fortnite is welcoming one and all to come in and try their Creative Mode and see where it brings them. You might be surprised to find what you come up with when you take the chance to express yourself. Have fun and then head out to where Battle Royale is being played and be a part of the matches when you're ready for heated combat. No matter how you want to play, you can do just that in Fortnite.

Everyone is having fun in Creative Mode and it is about time that you gave it a go, as well!

Do you think your island has what it takes to be featured on The Block? Do you think everyone is going to love how creative you are and how fun your game is? Now is your time to find out! Put your island together, set it as public and share with everyone else out there. You want to show off that talent, and you can with the powerful tools available to you and all of your creativity.

Start building the ultimate game today! The Block awaits your creation!

★★★ CREATE YOUR OWN MAP

When the time comes to play the game, you have an opportunity to impress with your creations, but first you have to think about how to do that. With Creative Mode everyone wants to bring to life exciting and impressive creations. They want to make custom games and show off their maps to their friends and even to random players. There are so many different features to work with that there's always something you can do to improve or alter your custom map. Follow these simple instructions and you'll be an expert builder in no time at all.

Of course, the first step to building an impressive map is to plan out its structure. Get an idea of what you want on your map and how it's all going to come together. Take time to draw your map out on paper and make a list of features you want on your map. Doing this will help ensure that you build the map you've always wanted. You'll also save time and build something that you can be proud of from the very beginning.

While building your own custom map, you can easily include all the features that you're most interested in. You'll feel great about your creation in the end if you work hard and do your best to build something impressive. There's nothing like the satisfaction of building your own custom world. It's even more exciting when others come to love your creations just as much as you do. When you're finally finished creating you can show off your builds, test them out with others and improve them over and over again.

Make sure to invite your friends out to try it first to perfect everything about your world. With enough work you might even get your game listed in The Block where thousands of other players will test it out!

WHAT TO PLACE ON YOUR MAP

From the moment you start playing Fortnite's Creative Mode, you'll likely be wondering just what you can put out on your map. It doesn't take long to get familiar with the interface, but you'll likely be overwhelmed with all the options available to you. Below we outline what you get access to in Creative, and how you can make the most of these different items while you craft your world. Read on and learn how to build something impressive.

Start with a Layout. Don't let all the different potential items overwhelm you when you start building your map on Creative Mode. Instead, draw up a plan to guide all your building. Take a minute to look through the different items, then sit down and think of what you would like to create in your own custom world. Finally, you should draw out a quick sketch of your world on paper. Use this to help build on your ideas, figure out what's possible and to give you a good starting point to work from. After you get all these foundations in place, you can do things like figure out how to make it all work and add in those finishing touches that will keep people wanting to come back again and again.

Screenshot © 2019, Epic Games, Inc.

CREATIVE   PLAY

Rare | Consumable

CASTLE

Place a building in an instant

Prefabs   Devices   Weapons   Consumables   Chest

Equip

Add to Chest

ESC Ba

With your idea in mind, or even if you just decide to wing it, it's time to start exploring the tools available, deciding on the pieces that you'll be building and adjusting your plans to pick the different building blocks you're going to use.

To start looking through tools and building blocks, head to the **inventory** that is located in the **backpack** icon on the right. This is where you will find everything you need to build and add. Also, with the **tab** button, you can create structures all your own if you choose – **ramps, walls, floors, stairs** and the normal building items that you use in the game can also be used in Creative Mode.

If you want to add buildings or other obstacles, you'll want to go to the **prefab** tab in the **backpack inventory.** Once you're there take inventory of the items you want to use most and make a list of them. Remember, you have a limited amount of resources available to build with, so choose with care!

The **prefab** tab provides the crafter with everything that they need to place in the game. All of the buildings are put together you just need to make sure they are placed right. If you need to place it and then switch it around from side to side, then you will want to use the **cell phone** to the right. With help from the phone tool you can accurately move, rotate and adjust every piece you lay down with precision.

Once you have your **prefabs** you are well on your way to creating an awesome map. However, there are some extras that you should know about because Creative Mode is about more than just **building** with an unlimited supply of crafting materials. You don't have to stop at laying down **prefab** buildings and setting up walls and floors. The **inventory** tool is a powerful editing utility you can use to adjust your creations to fit your needs exactly.

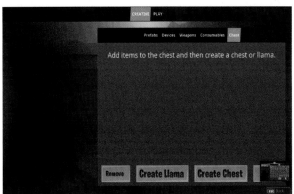

You can even **remove** the items from the **prefab** buildings and items that you put in the game. Just use the **cell phone** on the right-hand side and you're able to remove, change, add and do anything else you want to strip the buildings that you put into the game. This makes them more unique and more your own.

Powerful AR Phone Tools

The cell phone is one of the most important tools in Fortnite's Creative Mode, and it enables you to do use a bunch of different useful functions. Below is a quick list of the phone's features and what they will do for you in the game.

- **Copy –** Duplicate the current selection. This can be used to copy whole sections of a build reliably.

- **Push –** Move an object away from you efficiently.

- **Pull –** Move an object toward you.

- **Rotate –** Rotate a building clockwise or counter-clockwise.

- **Mirror –** Create's a flipped version of an item, like a mirror reflection.

- **Rotation Axis –** Switches how you rotate objects. Set rotate exactly the direction you want to adjust items with this feature.

- **Drops –** Used to turn gravity on and off for objects.

- **Grid Snap –** Used to precisely place objects on the map and to reposition them accurately.

Check Out the Other Things in the Inventory

You don't want to just let your imagination run without knowing what the inventory feature is capable of. Not only can you grab those prefab buildings, but you can create your own chests and piñatas! That's right, those piñatas and chests that you search so hard for in standard matches are available for you to place anywhere you like in this game mode!

Screenshot © 2019, Epic Games, Inc.

Simply select a piñata or a chest, and then start filling its inventory before you place it down. Once you build the inventory of one of these containers, you can put it anywhere you like in your game. Use them to supply teams for combat, or to hide supplies to get through your obstacle course. Whatever sort of experience you want to create in your Fortnite World, you can do just that with these valuable tools. To take full advantage of these containers, we strongly suggest waiting until your map and area is completely built out before you decide to add the chests and piñatas. By waiting you can get a better idea of what players will need, and what sort of weapons and tools you want to add around your map.

The best part about Creative Mode is that you can choose how much of the item to put into the game. If you're building a map for eight players and you don't want eight things in a chest, you can do that. One design decision will leave those players scrambling to find something. You can do that, you have complete control over how the players interact with your world. If you want them to have a surplus of things to choose from in a room full of weapons, you can do that too!

There are so many things you can do and with all of the options to choose from in the inventory, you don't have to worry about running out of options as you're creating. You really can do whatever you like. It's a powerful feeling!

Space Exit Fly (Double-Tap)

L-Shift Fly Up

L-Ctrl Fly Down

Tab Inventory

LEARNING SOME ADVANCED CONTROLS

There really isn't much to Creative Mode, but there are advanced controls make things a bit easier while you build. These controls are simple to use, but it might not be obvious how they work at first. That's why we break down the different tools and how you can use them down below.

Getting Objects to Float

Who hasn't thought about creating an awesome floating structure before? It's not obvious how to do this immediately, but it is possible to make items float on your map. If you want objects to float up in front of you and move the AR phone is the tool for you. Simply select

the **drop** option that is on the **G key.** If this is set to **on,** then the objects are going to fall to the ground when they are placed in the world. However, if you **turn it off,** then it is like turning off the gravity. Your creations will begin hovering in the air, and they even remain like that when gameplay starts.

Placing Objects an Even Amount of Space Apart

Getting things just so is harder to do than you think. It's important to make sure you have your structures laid out in the most effective manner, and that's where drawing up a layout first helps. If you're not interested in just plopping items down here and there while building, there are tools available to help you place items with precision.

Grid Snap is one of the most important features for placing buildings precisely. Use the **V key** to access this feature. Grid Snap is usually **set off** by default. But there are four settings that you can choose from depending on how precisely you want to lay down your objects. Choose one of the four options depending on how you want your buildings to interact as you place them down. You can select between a 2x2 grid, a 4x4 grid, an 8x8 grid

and finally a 16x16 grid. When you want space between objects a 2x2 grid is a good quick way to accomplish that goal evenly. When you want to lay objects with exact precision, the 16x16 grid lets you place them exactly where you like. Switch between the different grid settings to snap objects throughout the world exactly as you want them. It takes time to get comfortable with Grid Snap, but once you are familiar with the tool you'll never have trouble placing those objects perfectly again.

Toggling the Collision

If you want to choose whether or not the items can clip and collide with one another, you can do that using the collision setting. Press the V key in order to turn this setting on and off for different objects. This can help you when it comes to placing different items throughout the game.

When you know how to set up your own map, then you can make sure that anything happens that you want to happen. You don't have to worry about not being able to create the game the way you imagined it. You'll be amazed at how closely you can bring your ideas to life in Fortnite's new sandbox mode with just a bit of practice and proper planning.

After planning and building with care you shouldn't have any problems getting people to come in and play your game. With a little experience you can create something truly awesome. We know you can do it! Get started planning and practicing your builds and you'll be featured on The Block in no time!

Learn more about creating your own map below. With our walkthrough you'll be coming up with your own ideas in no time. We'll explain how to make a full game, instead of just adding random objects to your map without a plan.

**Are you ready to make the game playable?
Let's go!**

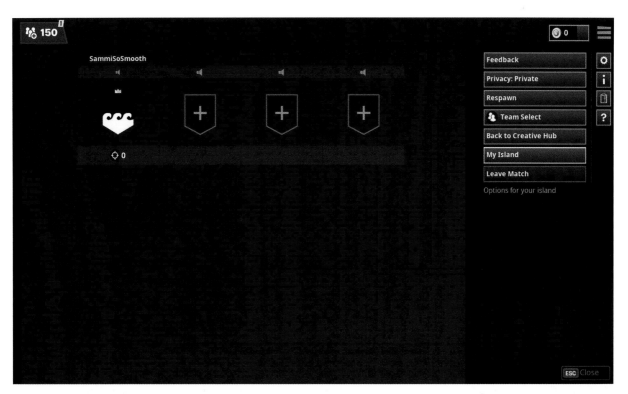

CREATING ON THE MAP

When you have your map laid out and you have your items where they need to go, it's time to focus on the actual gameplay experience in your world. While some worlds are designed for players to freely roam through them, with most you'll have a play experience in mind. With a Death Match, players will be battling one another. With an obstacle course, players will be moving through different obstacles. It's important you take steps to make sure that's what players will do when they reach your map. There are tools to make your game work properly.

There are controls that you can change to create the exact game that you have in mind. To get things set up press the **ESC button** and then go to the **My Island** option on the **menu** that pops down.

The first thing you have to think about when inside the menu is how many players you want in your world. You can have up to 16 different players in the game. Figure out that perfect number for your game. Often, it's best to have many players to increase the competition and fun, but other game modes like obstacle courses are better with fewer players.

Once done with player settings, you will want to choose which **game mode** works for you depending on the specific game type that you're building. There are many game types, and it's up to you to choose something that will work well with your game idea.

 71

MY ISLAND

GAME **GAME SETTINGS** **ISLAND TOOLS**

STARTING HEALTH	◄ FULL HEALTH ►
STARTING SHIELDS	◄ EMPTY SHIELDS ►
INFINITE AMMO	◄ OFF ►
INFINITE RESOURCES	◄ ON ►
PICK AXE BUILDING DAMAGE	◄ DEFAULT ►
DROP ITEMS WHEN ELIMINATED	◄ ON ►
FALL DAMAGE	◄ OFF ►
GRAVITY	◄ NORMAL ►
JUMP FATIGUE	◄ ON ►
PLAYER FLIGHT	◄ OFF ►

Restore Defaults   **APPLY**

GAME MODE

Start off by deciding on a Game Mode. You can choose Free Play for a free-roam style game, or elimination if you want your players to fight to the death.

TEAMS

Use the **teams option** to decide how players will interact in your game. Everyone can work together, or you can split them up into different team sizes. You can even have a **free for all,** where it is every man for himself. You can also pair up teams or do singles. There are many ways to make sure that you customize and make the game that you're creating your own and more geared towards the specific theme that you have.

With these settings you can do things like adjust. You are the one that sets the length of time that the game should last. The more time might mean that it can end quickly, or you may want them to scramble to win by giving them a shorter amount of time to beat.

MY ISLAND

| GAME | GAME SETTINGS | ISLAND TOOLS |

GAME MODE	◄	FREE PLAY	►
TEAMS	◄	FREE FOR ALL	►
TIME LIMIT	◄	5 MINUTES	►
SPAWNS	◄	2	►
LAST STANDING	◄	OFF	►
SPAWN LOCATION	◄	SPAWN PADS	►

*When the game completes your island will be restored
to its pre-game state*

Restore Defaults   **START GAME**

ESC | Close

ADJUSTING THE SPAWN SETTINGS

You can even choose where your players are going to **spawn** inside the game, which is important to making your game function properly. Elimination matches might have teams spawn in different locations to start the battle. Obstacle courses could have players spawn in a specific area of the map to begin. You can also set save points for something like an obstacle course, so players can save their progress as they work their way through your course.

When setting spawns you can choose whether players start in the sky or on a spawn pad. You can also choose the total number of spawns players get in your game, giving them limited lives if you like. You can even set the game to work as a last-man-standing game type just like Fortnite's own Battle Royale.

ESTABLISHING A TIME LIMIT

Some game types benefit from a time limit, while others should continue forever. Use the **Time Limit** setting to choose how long players have in your world before the game ends. You can force players to rush or give them the time to relax and make calculated decisions based on the time limits you set. Choose from unlimited time to a maximum of 20 minutes depending on the experience you're creating.

Once you have each of these settings adjusted the way you want them in the **Game Tab** it's time to move over to the **Game Settings** tab and adjust more settings that will affect how your visitors interact with the world even more.

ADJUSTING THE GAME SETTINGS

Game Settings are one of the most powerful ways you can control your world. You can use them to do everything from controlling player health, ammo, resources and shield power, to controlling the way the world functions. Below is an overview of the specific settings and what they do.

- **Starting Health –** Controls how much health players start with in your world. Go from full health down to 1 health or make players invincible.

- **Starting Shields –** Choose how much shield power players begin with. Choose no shields, half shields or full shields.

- **Infinite Ammo –** Turn this on to help players avoid searching for ammo.

- **Infinite Resources –** Players will have unlimited resources with this on.

- **Pick Axe Building Damage –** Controls how pickaxes damage buildings. Choosing Instant will let players one-hit walls and other structures for fast editing, or lightning quick battles.

- **Drop Items When Eliminated –** Choose whether player inventory drops to the ground at death with this option.

- **Fall Damage –** Turn fall damage on or off with this setting. Turning fall damage off might be essential for some obstacle courses.

- **Gravity –** Turn gravity up or down to create new experiences. You can even make players feel like they're floating around on the moon with the right settings.

- **Jump Fatigue –** When on, players jump lower and lower when jumping many times in a row. It prevents players from hopping constantly on your map.

- **Player Flight –** Choose whether players can fly or not.

- **Player Names and Location –** Decide who can see player names and locations. You can make it available to everyone, make the information available within teams, or keep everyone from seeing this information.

- **Respawn Height –** Choose how high players spawn above the ground from low to high after death.

- **Glider Redeploy –** Decides if players can use their glider again during the game or not. Another important consideration for different game types, especially obstacle courses.

- **Down But Not Out –** Determines whether players can be downed with the potential to be saved by team members before they are eliminated.

- **Building Damage in Game –** Determines if buildings can take damage and be destroyed.

- **Block Building in Game –** Control whether players can build or not in your world.

Use all these different settings to determine exactly how your game will work. With careful adjustments you can create a game that will run exactly the way you envisioned it.

TYPES OF MINI GAMES – FOR INSPIRATION

If you're wondering what exactly you should be making on your Island, it helps to plan, but it also helps to look at the creation of others.

Here are some of the most brilliant mini game ideas that we have come across, read through these ideas and you're sure to get inspired! Not only that, but if you want to adapt and create a map and game built off the premise that these provide, it can be an excellent way to create something compelling and really get people to come in and play.

One in the Chamber – You just have one bullet and you have to make the most of it. Make sure there are plenty of places to hide. With just one bullet each, players will make the most of their creativity to be the last one standing in the end.

Hide and Seek – In true old-fashioned ways, this is just as it seems, but with weapons and fighting. One player is the seeking, the rest are hiding. Just beware, because unlike regular hide and seek, when you are found, you're toast, and they are going to take you out. They are also the only ones with the guns, so make sure to run to the safe spot as soon as possible! Whoever is there when the game ends continues to the next round.

Spleef – We know, we know, it sounds weird, but it is fun. You build a large platform for one team and another for the other. Everyone shoots the other team's platform so that it breaks down. The wood will eventually give in and the team that is the last standing is the one that wins. It is a lot like playing Jenga, but in Fortnite, with weapons, on platforms. You get the idea.

Deathrun – A sniping tower is overlooking the course below where the players are going to be spending their time. You then create a course that the players have to get through. You can provide them with cover in certain areas, or with specific traps that might get them should they end up in those specific places. You can do one or two snipers with however many runners. The snipers work to take out the runners. The runners keep trying to make it through without getting killed and if they can do it, they become the sniper in the end. If they simply can't make it through the map the snipers are the winners.

Maze Runner — Just like the books, you need to be able to make it through the maze or you might get a worse fate than you can imagine. You and a friend or two teams of two people come together. One builds a maze on one side, with a platform in the middle and the others build another maze on the other side. Start in the middle, you have so long to build the maze for the other person. Once completed, you switch sides again and then you have to try to make it through the maze. Each maze has a hidden weapon in the middle of it. Reach the weapon and find your way back out to the base again and kill the opponent. First one that makes it and kills the other is the winner.

A Race Course — What fun would Fortnite Creative Mode be if you were not able to make a race course? Set up the game and then players choose wood, metal or brick and then they have to race through. The one that chooses wrong is the one that dies because it is the one that doesn't make it to the end of the track. It is all about luck and good times.

Rollercoaster Tycoon Fun – A shopping cart or ATK is needed for this one and you will ride around in this while hitting many different jump pads, bouncers and other things that shoot you into the air and then catch you as you come back down. This one is a pretty creative build because you don't have loops and spins that you go around.

Trick Shots – Someone is at the bottom of a platform, with another one or a few at the top. The person at the bottom uses a jump pad to snipe any of the players at the top of the platform. Take them all out or keep trying until it is someone else's turn. It becomes tricky because they can move if they want, you never know where they will be when you jump up.

Capture the Flag – You can do this game with set teams or 1v1. You would need a flag for each of the sides that are going to be playing the game. You will then want to make sure to have the same number of weapons on each side. The fewer weapons, the more challenging but definitely exciting the game can be. The teams have to try to steal the other team's flags and then bring them back safely to their base. Once they do, they are the winner.

Whether you want to use one of these neat ideas or come up with your own, you should be inspired to try to create something fun on one of your worlds.

Now is the time to really put everything together and show it off. Use our tool and setting explanations to get started. Use our tips below to help you create a map that you can be proud of.

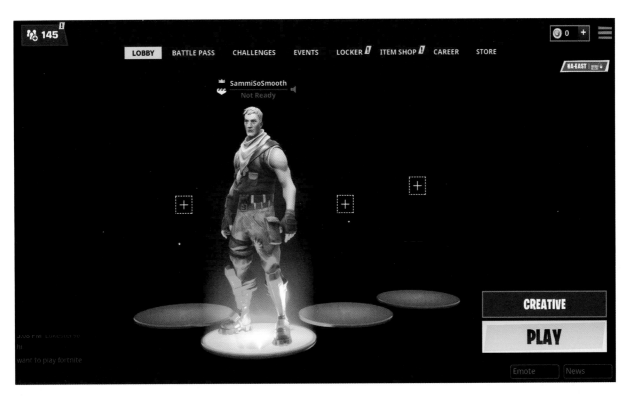

TIPS FOR CREATING YOUR MAP

There are going to be tips and tricks for just about everything that you do, so it is important that you think about some of the things that can either make your game awesome or might cause it to take a dive off the deep end. Make sure to keep these tips and tricks in mind when it comes to getting more from the games you put together and the map, you're creating full of excitement.

Of course, coming up with some super cool tricks of your own is also pretty awesome and definitely something you're going to want to share with your friends.

★ Plan out how you want your island to look before you start plopping things down. This will help you keep it organized and help dictate where to keep items.

★ Think about the type of game that you want to create and what you might need to create it and actually make it work.

★ You can theme the things that you build using the different buildings and items from the different places on the Fortnite map.

★ Remember that you have a specific amount of space and memory to use. The space on the island is only so wide, while the memory is only so large. The more items you put on your island, the more memory you're going to use to hold it there.

★ Make sure to do a few trial runs before releasing your island to the general public or submitting it for The Block. You want to make sure it looks right and is running perfectly. This means being able to have some friends come out and really tell you what they think of the entire thing.

★ Open the island up to your friends and have them tweak and move the things that they feel would benefit the overall look and feel of the island. When you work together, you can create great things that you might not have been able to create by yourself.

★ Remember, this is a game that you can fly in – so while creating the game, fly around and make sure to get a bird's eye view of the map and the game as you are putting it together. No need to run everywhere, this might take some time to get used to though.

★ Make sure to read through the whole guide so you know how to set the settings for the game and you know what to expect when it comes to setting up gameplay, the map and inviting players to come in, this is especially true if you don't want them doing anything to the map other than taking a look around. Permission settings are very important to consider.

★ Check out YouTube videos on some of the most awesome islands and games that were ever made by those that play this game. Even the most famous YouTube stars have created some pretty epic builds and are willing to allow everyone to show up and play with them – they might even give you the codes you need to enter in the video!

★ Fortnite has plenty of information on Creative Mode, how to use it, what to use, when to use it and more right from the Epic website, but if you want to listen to YouTubers, they have even enlisted a few of the top names like Ninja to provide everyone with some tutorials on using Creative Mode and what is in store for those that want to play.

★ Epic has stated that they will be updating Creative Mode throughout the years ahead, so you can expect to see many new items and layouts, as well as game modes and more to use while you play in this mode.

★ Remember! To join your friends on their islands or for you to have them join yours, you need to pass around the codes that are given for each. Everyone has a specific randomized code that was given to them when their island was originally made. This is used to get into every island.

Make sure that you are respectful of other players, the builds and the name Fortnite, because this is a game for everyone and you want to make sure that you and everyone else is having a good time.

Be graceful whether you win or lose a match. Also try and have a good time whether your creation is featured on The Block or not. You want to show everyone that you are cool with any sort of outcome and that you're a fun person to play with. You want to ensure that everyone else has a good time too.

Remain Safe While Playing

Epic is very good about keeping player information safe and secure on the servers and website. However, it is important that you don't provide this private information to anyone that you meet online. You want to keep your account and private information safe from these hackers.

You want to make this a great experience for one and all and when you follow the rules and keep up the fun, you won't have anything to worry about. Fortnite wants to make sure that everyone is using their creativity for good and with the help of all that comes with the game, you don't have to worry about what comes next. You're covered from start to finish.

Once you put together your map and your game and you know it is running like you want, then you should think about submitting the island into the section to become a part of Battle Royale's main map. This is a part of the map known as The Block. So many people want to be showcased here, but only the most loved creations will ever reach this coveted location. Anyone selected to take a spot on The Block is lucky and will have their creations viewed by thousands.

There's so much to do in Creative Mode that it's easy to forget something when making a map. Double check your creations before sending them off to The Block to be judged. Also, consider testing your creations out with others for ideas of ways you can improve. Do all these things and you'll come up with maps that you love and that you can have fun on again and again.

Players have even been talking to Fortnite trying to get them to support an idea for awarding vBucks to players with the most popular maps. That's a system that's already in place on Roblox, another popular online game. If the Fortnite creators decide to put some sort of vBucks system into Creative Mode, you'll benefit from having a high-quality map even more.

If this isn't an incentive to really think about the game that you're going to offer and the map you're going to make, then we don't know what would be!

START A
SERVER

FRIENDS OF FRIENDS

LAUNCH

CANCEL

What do you think could be added to this section of Fortnite to really make it stand out and be better, bigger and awesome-er than ever? We'd love to hear your take on the whole subject and we cannot wait to see those awesome **Fortnite creations up and shown off on The Block!**

If you were going to pay to visit a game world, what sort of features would you want it to have inside? That's the sort of question you need to ask yourself when making your world. What sort of features would make you willing to spend vBucks, and what's going to get your world noticed? Figure those things out and you'll be on your way to creating an impressive world.

PLAYER CREATIONS

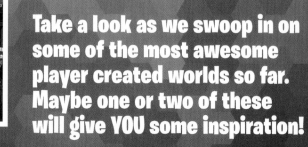

Take a look as we swoop in on some of the most awesome player created worlds so far. Maybe one or two of these will give YOU some inspiration!

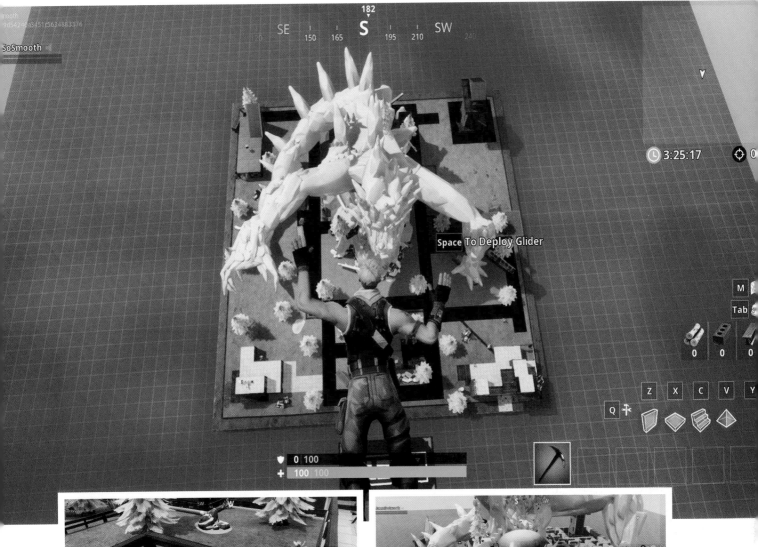

PRUDIZ'S WORLD

4351-4005-8292

COUNTLESS CRATES; GREAT SETUP

Have a box-full of laughs trying to find all the hidden crates on Prudiz's Island.

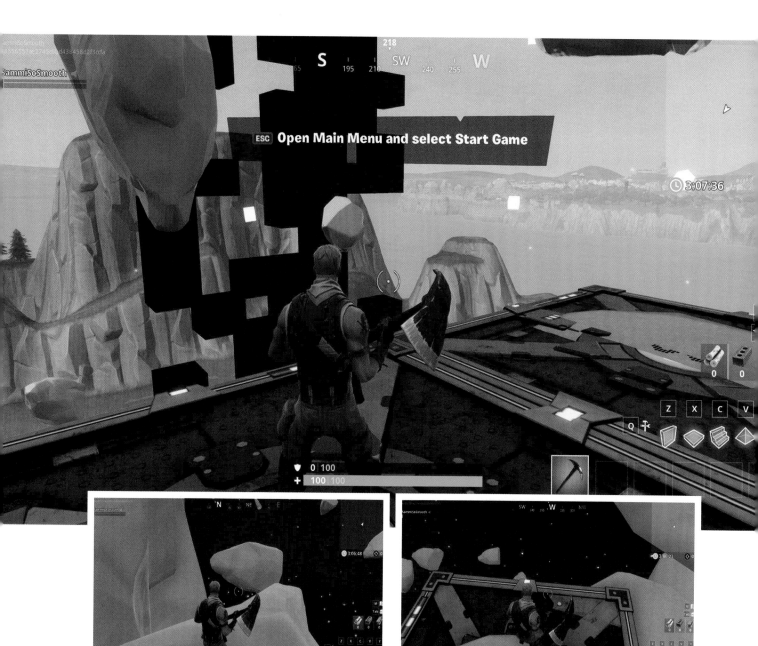

SPACE PARKOUR

1986-0450-3000

SPACE JAM

Mix some classic Mario and some floating meteors and skip through outer space in this cool setup.

Build your own Fortnite! Everything you do here is saved.

LAKESHORE LODGE

6585-8238-0391

WINTER WONDERLAND

Hit the slopes, enjoy the apres ski, and more at the Lakeshore Lodge.

LOOMING LLAMA

6388-1013-6876

DRAMA LLAMA

If you simply can't get enough of llamas in your gaming (like us!) then the giant structure looming large over you in this world will give you a Whole Llama Love.

RAINBOW ROAD

2668-3299-2351

I'M A GONNA WIN!

Rev up your engine for this world that bears a strong resemblance to classic kart racing games for video game consoles.

ESCAPE THE DREAM

5496-4876-0626

GET OUT

Imagine mixing an escape room experience with Fortnite, and you have one of the most compelling and exhilarating worlds we've seen yet.

HIDE & SEEK MAP
1466-2200-5392

OLLIE, OLLIE

Everyone loves a good game of hide and seek, and this world delivers a world with many ingenious hiding places. Set a time limit for extra fun!

MARBLE MALL

5266-7624-0602

SHOPPING SPREE

We can probably all agree the one thing Fortnite really needed was a shopping mall. Need to settle a score? Hit the Marble Mall for some merch *and* mayhem.

MAHAL MUSEUM

1512-9091-3630Halo

CALLING DR. JONES?

Sift through dusty artifacts, topple musty relics, and find clues to unlock mysteries buried for thousands of years in this mock museum map.

TINKER'S TOYSTORE

0632-6317-2480

TOYS, TARGETS & TNT

Depending on who you are, there is nothing worse (or better) than browsing through a charming toy store, trying new games or checking out the dolls and stuffed animals, when a full-on Fortnite firefight breaks out.

HALO'S LOCKOUT

9587-6651-4676

HECK YEAH, IT'S HALO!

The rumors are true: a Halo map in Fortnite! If you're a fan of Master Chief visit this world and get an extra edge on your competition.

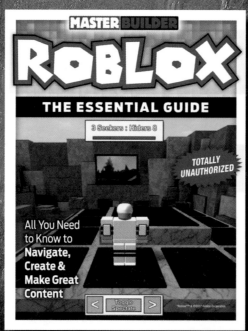